Abbotsbury & the Swannery

A nineteenth century engraving of the Swanherd feeding the swans.

FOLLOWING PAGE *Abbotsbury from Jubilee Coppice.*

JOHN FAIR AND DON MOXOM
PHOTOGRAPHS BY PEYTO SLATTER

THE DOVECOTE PRESS

Abbotsbury & the Swannery

First published in 1993 by The Dovecote Press Ltd
Stanbridge, Wimborne, Dorset BH21 4JD

ISBN 1 874336 07 5 (casebound)
ISBN 1 874336 08 3 (paperback)

Designed by Humphrey Stone

Photoset in Sabon by The Typesetting Bureau Ltd, Wimborne, Dorset
Origination by Chroma Graphics (Overseas) Pte Ltd, Singapore
Printed and bound by Kim Hup Lee Printing Co Ltd, Singapore

British Library Cataloguing-in-Publication Data
A catalogue record of this book is
available from the British Library

Contents

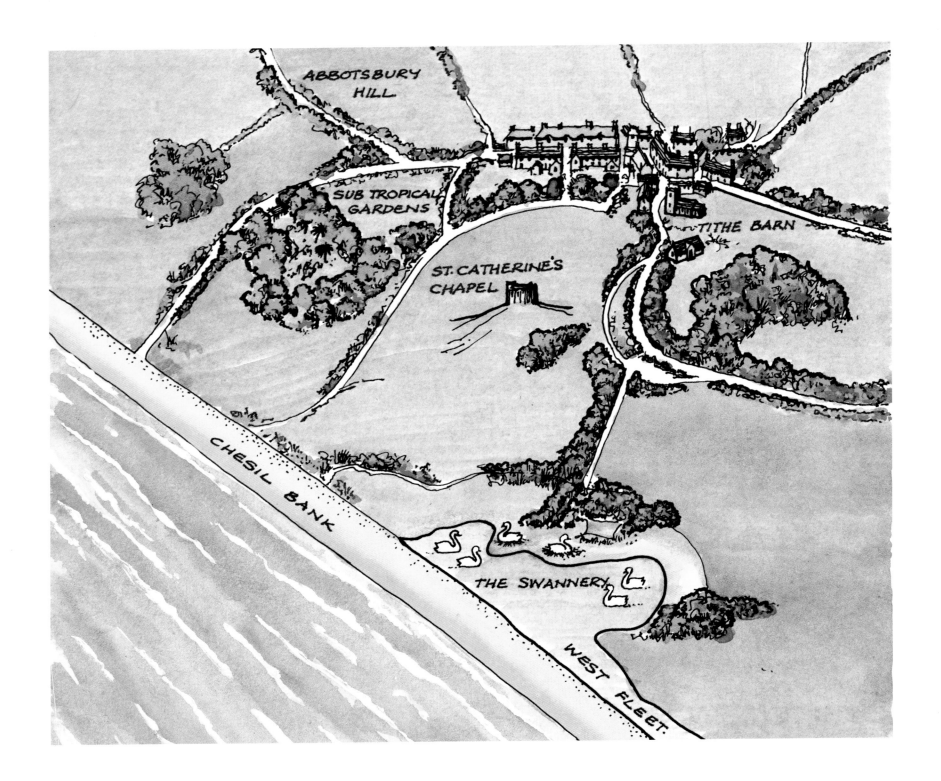

Foreword

Nearly five hundred years ago, in 1505, Thomas Strangways was buried in the Abbey of St Peter, Abbotsbury. Half a century later, following the Dissolution of the Monasteries, Thomas's son bought the Abbey buildings, the Swannery and the surrounding land. The two events marked the beginning of a link between Abbotsbury and my family that has endured for fifteen generations, during which time we have tried to preserve and enhance the area.

Such continuity is rare, but easily understood. Few villages in Dorset enjoy a more beautiful setting. The view from Abbotsbury Hill along the eight mile length of the Chesil Beach towards the Isle of Portland is one of the finest in England.

From all aspects, from the Tithe Barn, the Sub-tropical Gardens, the thatched cottages in the village to St Catherine's Chapel, it is very evident what makes Abbotsbury so special.

It's most famous attraction is undoubtedly the Swannery. It was first mentioned in 1393, six centuries ago, and remains a unique and fascinating link with the medieval monks. It is perhaps fitting that the authors of this book, John Fair and Don Moxom, should be involved in the management and preservation of the wildlife on the Fleet and Chesil Bank. Peyto Slatter's colour photographs are a superb evocation of not only this but Abbotsbury as a whole.

Each year many thousands of visitors come to Abbotsbury, and I hope that this book will help to explain why.

Charlotte Morrison

THE HONOURABLE MRS MORRISON

ERIC RICKETTS
'92.

Early and Monastic Abbotsbury

The medieval monks who planted their crops in the strip fields around Abbotsbury weren't the first to farm the area. Originally it had been covered with dense woodland, which was gradually cleared from about 6000 years ago. Nomadic tribesmen grazed their livestock along the shore of the Fleet. Later, during the Bronze Age (2,300 BC - 700 BC), seventeen burial barrows were built on top of the ridge to the north of the village. These were burial places of important people, perhaps chieftains.

In the following Iron Age (700 BC - AD 43) a hillfort known as Abbotsbury Castle was built on Wears Hill to the north-west of the village. Its double ramparts enclose four acres and are still visible today. Inside are the outlines of a group of circular huts once entered along narrow passages that face, in unison, away from the prevailing south-westerly winds. The hillfort was the main settlement in the area, and was where every one gathered in times of danger.

There is no Roman occupation known round Abbotsbury, though with the Roman town of Durnovaria (Dorchester) so close it seems almost certain that they settled in the area. The first mention of the name is in a land grant of the 10th century, six hundred years after the Roman withdrawal. As to the monastery, Thomas Gerard writing in 1625 recorded a tradition that it was built 'in the verie infancie of Christianitie amongst the Britains' by a priest called Bertufus, to whom Saint Peter is supposed to have appeared, even giving him a charter 'written with his owne Hande.' It is a good story, but not even Gerard believed it.

The monastery was really founded in the 11th century by Orc and his wife Tola. They were followers of King Canute who was King of Denmark, Norway and part of Sweden as well as England, and like him were Vikings. Orc was the king's steward, and was given the land by Canute. There already was a church at Abbotsbury, but constant pillage had led to its being abandoned.

LEFT *A reconstruction of what the great Benedictine Abbey at Abbotsbury probably looked like, with the parish church of St Nicholas beside it. The remains of the two gatehouses in the foreground are still standing today.*

RIGHT *Dorset's oldest surviving document, part of King Canute's Charter granting land at Abbotsbury to Orc in 1023.*

An eighteenth century engraving of the original medieval Abbey watermill, which though altered still stands and is now known as the Old Malthouse.

The exact date of the monastery's foundation remains uncertain, but it was probably in the 1040s, twenty or so years before the Norman Conquest. Orc outlived Canute and became Edward the Confessor's steward as well, and it was Edward who granted him the sea shore bordering his lands and the right to all wrecks – both unusually high honours. Orc was buried in the monastery he founded. Seven hundred years later, in the 17th century, Gerard saw his bones 'inclosed in a daintie Marbill Coffin' in the parish church, but they have since disappeared.

In due course the monastery became one of the wealthiest in Dorset. Besides the whole village of Abbotsbury with its weekly market and 2,000 acres in the parish, it owned lands in twelve other parishes and houses in Wareham, Bridport and Dorchester. The present church of St Nicholas was on one edge of the monastery and was always the separate parish church, for the use of the villagers not the monks. The church of St Peter served the monastery and was immediately to the south, but has completely disappeared. It was nearly as long as the Tithe Barn and had cloisters and a chapter house attached. The Abbey enclosure ran south from the church across the little river valley, but only a few of the buildings survive. Below the church is what is known as the 'Pynion End', the gable end of a large building once perhaps joined to the cloisters. To the east are the mill and what was once the Abbot's Lodging, whilst the remains of two gatehouses can be seen alongside the lane to the west. The most impressive building is the Tithe Barn. It was built in about 1400 and was originally 270 feet long. Only half remains roofed, but its size alone provides some idea of how rich the Abbey must once have been.

Medieval monasteries were like any other large medieval landowner. The monastery would have been self-sufficient, grinding its own corn, breeding swans for the table in the Swannery, pigeon in the pigeon house that still stands near the Tithe Barn, fattening carp in its fishponds, growing its own vegetables and herbs. Lay brothers did much of the heavy work, whilst the monks participated in a daily cycle of services in the church. There were medieval manuscripts to illuminate, a skill for which Abbotsbury was renowned. Masses had to be sung for the dead in the chantry chapels that added to the abbey's revenues. Abbotsbury was Benedictine, so the brothers wore black habits and divided their day into five hours of prayer, five of manual work, and four reading the Scriptures.

Little is known directly about the monks. One 14th century abbot died from the Black Death. Another was criticised for keeping hunting dogs and too many servants, as well as not attending services and refusing to eat with the other monks in the refectory. These accusations pale beside those made (probably unjustly) about the last abbot, Roger Hardie, who was accused of stealing jewels and plate, selling woodland, and the 'kepying of women, nott wyth one or two or three but wyth manie more'. The attack on Abbot Hardie probably had more to do with the events leading up the abbey's dissolution than anything else. Like every other monastic house in Dorset, Abbotsbury was not immune to Henry VIII's determination to force their closure and sale. It was finally dissolved in 1539, when its annual income was just over £400. They were only nine monks, and Abbot Hardie became vicar of Abbotsbury, moving from the huge church of St Peter to the smaller parish church next door.

RIGHT *The Tithe Barn, built in about 1400 and once 270 feet long. The half that remains roofed is now a Country Museum.*

BELOW *The twelfth century effigy of one of the abbots, now in the church porch.*

Because so few of the monastic buildings remain, the best clue to the wealth and prestige once enjoyed by the abbey is St Catherine's Chapel. Sitting on its domed hill, surrounded by the narrow medieval fields cut into the hillside, it still dominates the Abbotsbury landscape. Remarkably, it is built entirely of local stone, from its foundations to the stone-slabbed slates on the roof. It survives because of its importance as a seamark to sailors crossing the dangerous waters of Lyme Bay. St Catherine is the patron saint of spinsters, who one day a year can pray in the chapel for a husband:

> A Husband, St Catherine,
> A handsome one, St Catherine,
> A rich one, St Catherine,
> A nice one, St Catherine.
> And soon, St Catherine.

Or better still, in Dorset dialect:

> Sweet St Catherine send me a husband.
> A good one I pray.
> But arn-a-one better than narn-a-one
> Oh St Catherine, Lend me thine aid,
> And grant that I never may die an old maid.

OPPOSITE *St Catherine's Chapel in the mist.*

ABOVE RIGHT *The gateway, a remnant of the house built by Sir Giles Strangways and destroyed in the Civil War, frames an even older remnant, the 'Pynion End', left standing since 1539.*

RIGHT *The parish church of St Nicholas dominates this view of the village. Note the dovecote in the field in the background.*

*St Catherine's Chapel survived the Abbey's dissolution because of its
importance as a sea-mark to sailors crossing Lyme Bay. The strip lynchets
highlighted in the evening shadows are known as the 'Chapel Rings'.*

14

Abbotsbury and the Ilchester Family

The alabaster effigy of Sir Giles Strangways in the church at Melbury Sampford shows a thickset sturdy figure, dressed in full armour, his head resting on a helmet, hands pressed together in prayer above his breastplate. It is a fitting image, neatly combining the mixture of piety and single-mindedness needed to prosper in Tudor England.

For like many of the Commissioners appointed by Henry VIII to administer the surrender of the monasteries, Sir Giles wasted little opportunity in profiting from their misfortunes. Four years after enforcing the closure of the Abbey of St Peter, Abbotsbury, he bought it, paying £1,906 10s for the buildings, its manor, more than 2000 acres of land, two mills, and the Swannery. It was an astute purchase, but even he could surely not have imagined that fifteen generations and nearly five hundred years later both Abbotsbury and the Swannery would still belong to his descendants.

The Strangways had come south from Yorkshire towards the end of the 15th century, settling at Melbury Sampford, a small village north of Dorchester on the western edge of the Blackmore Vale. Abbotsbury was 20 miles south, and Sir Giles's decision to acquire the Abbey was surely influenced by the fact that his father had been buried there in 1505, and that the family had founded a chantry at the Abbey which paid for a priest to say a daily mass for his father's soul. A condition of Abbotsbury's

purchase was the dismantling and removal of the monastic buildings. Sir Giles built or adapted a house for himself out of part of them, and much of the stone of the rest was incorporated into cottages in the villages. Some fragments of decoratively carved stone can be seen above doorways and windows.

By the seventeenth century any advantage gained by the change of landlord must have seemed slight to the villagers. Abbotsbury was described as being 'but poore, the chiefest trade consists in fishing.' The outbreak of the Civil War in 1640 brought yet greater hardships. Abbotsbury was then owned by Sir John Strangways, an ardent Royalist and supporter of Charles I. The first hint of what lay ahead took place in April 1643 when the family house in the village was occupied by a detachment of Parliamentary troops. When Sir John's wife, Grace, refused to co-operate the house was ransacked.

A year later, in November 1644, a larger Parliamentary force under Sir Anthony Ashley Cooper marched south from Dorchester determined to rid the village of its Royalist garrison, then commanded by one of Sir John's sons, Colonel James Strangways. Ashley Cooper first stormed the church, and the scars of the battle that followed can still be seen in the holes made by musket shots in and around the pulpit.

With the church safely taken, Ashley Cooper asked Strangways to surrender the house, which he refused to do. The six hour battle that followed was, to quote a member of the attacking force, 'as hot a storm as ever I heard of'. Ashley Cooper's men were forced to burn down a small gatehouse in order to reach the house. They then set fire to the entrance porch, simultaneously

LEFT *The interior of the parish church of St Nicholas. Bullet holes made by the Parliamentarians when they stormed the church in 1644 are still visible in the pulpit.*

Sir John Strangways (1584-1666), owner of Abbotsbury during the Civil War and later imprisoned in the Tower of London for his loyalty to Charles I.

keeping up a constant fusillade of musket fire that forced the garrison to stay upstairs. Meanwhile a second Parliamentary force used grenades, fire-balls and scaling ladders to reach the second floor windows at the rear. Wrenching open the windows, they tossed in bundles of burning faggots, setting the entire house ablaze and forcing the garrison to surrender. The victorious besiegers began ransacking the house, despite warnings that some barrels of powder might explode any minute. The inevitable happened, and is best described by Ashley Cooper in the vivid account of the action he wrote later: 'for the powder taking fire blew up all that were in the house . . . We had hurt and killed by the enemy not fifteen, but I fear four times that number will not satisfy for the last mischance.'

Sadly, the house was completely destroyed by the fire, as were all but a handful of the original monastic records and charters.

In the wake of the battle, Colonel James Strangways escaped to France, but both his father and elder brother, Giles, were captured after the Siege of Sherborne in 1645 and imprisoned in the Tower. Pleading his 'age and infirmities', Sir John was released three years later, though Giles was held hostage close to London until the family had paid a £10,000 fine. Altogether the family's support for the crown was to cost them £35,000, perhaps 20 million in modern money. Despite such sacrifices, the family's loyalty was unshakeable, and Giles gave Charles II £100 in gold when he was in hiding and trying to escape to France after the Battle of Worcester – a gift later described as 'the most seasonable present the Royal fugitive ever received'.

Red Valerian and daisies flowering in the churchyard in summer.

A drawing by Samuel Grimm of the Tithe Barn and village in the late eighteenth century. Note the haystacks in the churchyard.

As the 18th century dawned it must have seemed to the villagers who had lived through the Civil War that Abbotsbury's misfortunes were unending. For in 1706 the entire western end of the village burned down. Its two annual fairs were a thing of the past, and it largely depended for its survival on farming, fishing, and the spinning of cotton yarn for stockings. Only the sea offered an easier if illegal way of earning a living. The London Journal of 1752 claimed that 'All the people of Abbotsbury, including the Vicar, are thieves, smugglers and plunderers of wrecks'. The village's fortunes began to revive in the mid-18th century following the marriage of Elizabeth Strangways Horner to the influential Stephen Fox, later the 1st Earl of Ilchester. It was Elizabeth who built the ill-fated Abbotsbury Castle as a summer home, and began the gardens that still flourish today. For the next 150 years, until the fire which gutted the Castle in 1913, early summer saw a procession of heavily-laden carts, waggons and carriages trundling along the lanes between Melbury and the coast when the family moved to Abbotsbury for the summer.

The village's links with the rest of Dorset gradually grew stronger. The medieval strip fields were enclosed. Toll roads to both Bridport and Weymouth were opened. Cottage industries such as basket and rope-making brought both modest prosperity and a rise in population which reached a high-water mark of 1089 in 1861.

The village's long-term future must have seem assured with the opening of the railway from Weymouth in 1885. Interestingly, the prospectus mentions the Swannery as a potential tourist attraction, though the railway's main purpose was to transport iron ore from open-cast quarries in the hills behind the village.

The project was a failure from the outset. The railway was never profitable, finally closing in 1952.

In 1880 Abbotsbury supported two blacksmiths, bakers, bootmakers, grocers, wheelwrights and tailors, as well as a saddler, cooper, miller and butcher. Within fifty years both that list and its population had more than halved. One World War lay in the past, another loomed on the horizon. The village still belonged to the Estate, but those responsible for managing it must have feared that a decline had begun that could never be halted.

Yet as Abbotsbury draws towards the end of the 20th century it is obvious that its assets outweigh its size and it can face the future with optimism. The careful restoration of many of the cottages during the 1970s led to a Conservation Award in 1975, European Architectural Heritage Year. New recently-built stone and thatch cottages are the perfect example of what can still be achieved by a sympathetic architect and enlightened landowner. Few would question Abbotsbury's attractions. The Swannery, Sub-tropical Gardens and Tithe Barn would alone place it near the top of any list of Dorset's most beautiful villages. But it is also a living community, and one whose future will undoubtedly be shaped by the rich heritage of its past.

TOP *Market Street and West Street in about 1910.*

ABOVE *Abbotsbury Station in 1907.*

RIGHT *Recently-built stone and thatch cottages in Back Street.*

20

ABOVE *Villagers in the garden of their cottage in Rodden Row.*

RIGHT *The village from Rope Walk, with the Manor House on the left and the Dairy House, once one of the monastic gatehouses, on the right.*

ABOVE *James Kidd-Brown at work in his mason's yard, a link with a tradition that goes back to the fragments of ornamental stone carving from the medieval Abbey that can still be seen on various buildings around the village.*

TOP LEFT *Care is taken to use local materials when building new houses so that they blend in with the rest of the village.*

LEFT *Ashley Arnold belongs to an old Abbotsbury family, and rope and net-making have long been important cottage industries in the village. Most of Ashley's work today is repairs to sports nets, including tennis nets from Wimbledon.*

OPPOSITE PAGE *A cricket match in progress at the foot of Chapel Hill.*

ABOVE *Feeding the ducks on Tithe Barn Pond.*

ABOVE RIGHT *April Cottage.*

RIGHT *The old basket-maker's shop. The same building in 1925, with the basket-maker at work outside it, can be seen on page 57.*

OPPOSITE PAGE *Tithe Barn Pond. The house behind the thatched cottage was originally one of the Abbey gatehouses.*

The Swannery

The true origins of the Abbotsbury Swannery are lost in the dim mists of the past, but it is first mentioned in 1393. It occurs in the most unlikely of places, a long roll of sheep or goat skins sewn into strips with sheep sinews. These strips formed the Monks' Court Rolls and were the record of wrongs adjudicated upon by the Abbot. The entry in question refers to the 7d fine imposed on William Squillor, the monastery Swanherd, for lowering some hatches or sluice boards and flooding the nest site at nesting time by raising the water level in the Fleet – something we occasionally but accidentally still do.

Although we have no written proof of the existence of the Swannery prior to 1393 it seems certain that a colony of Mute swans had been nesting in the Fleet long before that date. Indeed, it seems probable that the swans were already there when the monastery was founded in the 11th century, and that the monks merely took advantage of their presence, and potential, as a source of food and income.

The Mute swan itself is certainly much older than the monastery, and its fossilised bones dating back to the Ice Age have been found in Cambridgeshire. It owes its name to the lack of a loud call, and those at Abbotsbury are more properly described as the Abbotsbury Colonial Nesting Herd. The word 'Colonial' comes from the fact that they nest close together. Some argue that they did this for protection, as wolves roamed the country at one time, but I think it more likely that they were forced to do so because suitable areas for nesting have always been scarce. Mute swans need flat land with streams, as well as reed for nesting material. A thousand swans winter on the Fleet, and the nesting

The section of the Monks' Court Roll of 1393 incorporating the first known mention of the Swannery, and a modern translation. The Roll is made of strips of sheep or goats-skins sewn together with sinews.

The East Tithing Presents that William Squilor Keeper of the Swans, stirred up the water under the bridge "a la Flete" with "Les hacches" so that the water overflowed in "Le Flete" and was so high that it washed against the nests of the Swans of the Lord and moved and destroyed the eggs of the Swans.
By the default of the same William. Therefore he is in mercy.

site is only five acres. They must either nest close to one-another, or not at all. Having said this, the stronger and more experienced pairs can successfully use their wings to beat away foxes trying to steal their eggs.

As well as providing the medieval monks with fresh meat, the swans' wing quills were used for writing and pillows were stuffed with their down. At one time the Fleet was known as 'Anglice a Meare', from the old French word 'Anglicing', meaning 'pinioning' or the removal of part of the wing. This was presumably done so that some swans could be penned and fattened for the table. Today, of course, they are no longer eaten, but they still have their uses. Lloyds of London use Abbotsbury quills to enter shipping and other insurance losses in their 'Doom' Book. The white headpieces on the helmets of the Queen's bodyguard, the Gentleman at Arms, are made up from the soft feathers under the wings of the Abbotsbury swans. Several hundred feathers are needed for each helmet, and we still supply sufficient to complete one a year.

Legally, all swans at large on open water today belong to the Queen. The only exceptions are the Abbotsbury Herd and those on the Thames belonging to the Worshipful Company of Vintners and Dyers. The ownership of the Abbotsbury Herd by the Abbey ended with its dissolution in 1539, and it was acquired by the Strangways family when they bought both the village and estate. To show ownership by the family, the swans are nicked with a sharp knife on the outside of the web. This mark is called the 'Hive of Ilchester', from an old word for an indentation, and possibly refers to a series of small inlets along the back of the Fleet: Rodden Hive, Langton Hive, Chickerel Hive. As well as marking the swans, they are also ringed with numbered white rings – mainly because all Mute swans look alike and we need to be able to identify them. The presence of the Fleet, the eight mile long brackish lagoon tucked behind the Chesil Bank, is crucial to the continued survival of Mute swans at Abbotsbury – without it, there would be no colony. Each swan consumes about eight pounds of plant food a day, and the Fleet's shallow waters are rich in the lush underwater 'meadows' of eel grass on which they feed. All the birds on the Fleet are free to come and go as they please, but food is so plentiful that in winter swans from other

A 'Reward' notice of 1830. Abbotsbury's swans have always been carefully protected.

places gather on its waters. Some breed with the Ilchester birds, and some join the colony. Thanks to the rings, the extent to which this happens has only recently come to light. Most of these young swans reach maturity with little human interference, just as they would elsewhere. Only at breeding time are they helped and 'managed'.

Responsibility for the Abbotsbury Herd lies with the Swan-herd, as it has done since time immemorial. Only occasionally do we have a record of their names, as in 1591 when Queen Elizabeth I claimed 410 swans and 90 cygnets because the Swan-herd had not marked them. So valuable were swans then that Dorset's High Sheriff was despatched to Abbotsbury to acquire them for the crown. Perhaps the best known of recent Swanherds is Fred Lexster, who died in 1982. Fred was a born raconteur and highly knowledgeable about the Fleet and its inhabitants. He was well-known for his radio and television broadcasts, and for his long association with Ludwig Koch, the first person to seriously record bird songs.

The Mute swan is one of the world's two heaviest flying birds, but temperamentally those at Abbotsbury are only rarely aggressive. The natural territorial instinct of those in the colony doesn't stop them accepting human beings. Total strangers can walk round the nesting site without being threatened by anything other than the occasional warning hiss not to touch either the eggs or young. Curiously, the staff aren't treated so lightly, perhaps because the swans expect us to handle their young. All the swans can pick us out, even from amongst a crowd and despite the fact that we often wear different clothes. We know that they can recognize voice patterns, but they can even distinguish us when we approach without talking, and show their aggression by forming a roof shape with their wings. It takes the newly hatched young about ten days to recognize us, as long as it takes to fully learn their own parents' calls. They then lift their heads when we approach, a sign of recognition meaning 'we know who you are, you bring food, you are good news'. Non-breeding birds give the same head lift, but theirs means that though they recognize us they don't necessarily like us.

This behaviour can at times be very amusing. Visitors are sometimes intimidated by a swan standing in the middle of the path, wings up, neck feathers fluffed out, and drawing himself up to exaggerate his size. Scared of moving forward, the visitor then fetches a member of the staff, whose arrival merely adds to the bird's aggressiveness and can lead to it hitting out. This of course frightens the visitor even more. Time then has to be spent persuading the visitor to go ahead and walk quietly forward, which is even more difficult, as they then think it is us who are afraid! Thanks to the numbers on the rings, we can work out the ages of the birds. Fifteen is a good age, and our oldest survivor is

Fred Lexster, or 'Leckie'.

A female swan, or pen, with her cygnets on the water.

a sixteen year old female, though the record stands at twenty-five. Contrary to popular belief, swans elsewhere in England are not always faithful to one partner, and divorce and wife-swapping are common. One would think that this would be the same at Abbotsbury, where over a thousand birds are resident in the winter. Curiously however, the majority of the Abbotsbury herd remain paired for life, something else we have learned since starting ringing in 1975.

Management of the herd really begins at nesting time. We record the position of the nest on a map, the ring number of each breeding pair, the date each egg is laid, and the date it hatches. When the cygnets are two days old, and dry and fluffy, but before their parents first lead them to the water, each is given a small numbered web tag. This helps considerably, as cygnets easily become confused and lost in so big a colony. As Swanherd, I then have to decide whether to return them to their parents, or

foster them elsewhere. This can depend on a number of things – the distance to water from the nest, how good the parents are at looking after their young, and how many other swan territories the family has to walk through on its daily journeys to and from the water. To make their progress to the Fleet even easier, we sometimes actually walk with them.

One way of helping the families who in recent years have begun nesting further from the Fleet is to feed them in temporary troughs, which also saves them having to run the gauntlet of other birds' territories. This is done three times a day, an immense amount of work, as it means carrying food and water to over a hundred nests. Even with this additional molly-

BELOW *Gregory Gill, the Swanherd in 1890.*

RIGHT *The Swannery nesting site on the edge of the Fleet, with the Decoy Pond in the foreground and the Chesil Bank and open sea in the distance.*

coddling, only a hundred or so cygnets survive out of six times that number of eggs.

The least successful at breeding are newly-paired swans and young birds nesting for the first time. To relieve the pressure on the territories some of the earliest families to hatch are put in pens. These are usually the most dominant and well-established. By removing them, space is created round their now empty nesting area, making a new territory in which pairs nesting later can fight for dominance. Birds usually accept being moved, and at the same time they can be given extra cygnets to foster. Families with less than three cygnets are never chosen, as we think the adults can count up to three and they are unwilling to take on the burden of looking after extra young.

Despite the casualties, the recent mild winters have added to the survival rate. The national swan population has increased by forty-two percent since the last census in the 1980s. The 133 pairs of swans nesting at Abbotsbury in 1991 managed to rear 142 cygnets. A hard winter though can easily bring tragedy in its wake. Many hundreds of swans died on the Fleet during the severe winter of 1962-63, and well over a hundred during 1986.

As winter progresses, particularly during February, plant food becomes harder to find. Other birds as well as the Abbotsbury swans over-winter on the Fleet. Their numbers are immense. So popular is the Fleet, that up to 20,000 other waterfowl spend part of their winters feeding on it – a total which includes nearly 9,000 wigeon, mostly from Russia, and 2,500 Brent geese from Siberia.

To relieve the pressure on the plant food, we scatter wheat in the water in early spring at a spot about a mile from the Swannery. Swans are all different, with individual characters, and some don't like being too near humans. The wheat leaves a larger share of the natural food available to both the more nervous swans and their over-wintering guests.

The well-being of the Abbotsbury herd is our prime concern, and the best way of checking its health is by rounding up every swan every two years. The 'Round Up' takes place in July, when the birds are moulting and unable to fly. Some 116,000 feathers have to be changed annually, a process that takes six weeks and amongst the first to be shed are the 'quills', or flight feathers.

The 'Round Up' is a vast operation. The staff are joined by some sixty people from the Wildfowl Trust, the Edward Grey Institute of Field Ornithology at Oxford, and other field workers. On the day before, we quietly drive the swans from the eastern end of the Fleet using canoes and boats. To prevent them swimming back down the Fleet, we make a barrier using the canoes or part of our oil boom, hemming them in in the Swannery bay at Shipmoor Point, where the Fleet narrows to a couple of hundred yards.

At dawn on the following day the 'net' of boats is carefully moved towards a prepared and cleared area of land west of the nest site. It is no easy task, as every swan swims to and fro in

ABOVE *Making home is a joint effort: the gentleman gathers the materials, the lady makes it just so!*

FOLLOWING PAGE *A general view of the nesting site in spring.*

TOP *During the five week incubation period the cob faithfully guards his mate and will take his turn at sitting on the eggs so she can feed and stretch her legs.*

BOTTOM *Newly-hatched cygnets.*

OPPOSITE PAGE *A swan with her cygnets.*

search of escape. Other helpers jump in the water to complete the 'net' and the whole thing – boats, people, swans – moves gradually closer to the land. One year the net was so effective we all but drove a hundred mullet ashore, which meant we finished the 'Round Up' with fish swimming between our legs! The aim is to round up every swan, but there are always some who have completed the moult and manage to get airborne and escape. The Abbotsbury 'Round Up' is unique, and usually involves 650 to 800 birds.

Once the swans are penned behind wire netting they tend not to panic, but stand quietly until caught. Every bird is then individually hand-held and checked for wounds or a broken ring, as a cracked ring can easily work its way down over a bird's foot and cause damage. We usually find some hundred or so birds without a ring at all. These are given a yellow ring on one leg and a metal British Trust for Ornithology ring on the other, though twice since 1980 I have been confronted with birds with only one leg!

Some people disapprove of ringing, but it has been a major factor in enabling us to build up a picture of the private life of the Mute swan, and the not-so private life of the Abbotsbury herd. Rings mean we know a swan's age, where they breed, how many mates each has during its life. Rings were also vital to identifying the areas where lead poisoning from fish weights was occuring, something that wasn't known until 1980, when lead poisoning was annually causing the death of 3,000 swans. That year we collected a piece of egg shell from many of the nests, which were then analysed for lead content. As Abbotsbury swans have less lead in their system than elsewhere in Britain, scientists were able to work out how much lead a swan can absorb before it dies and help swans in other areas.

Thus the 'Round Up' has a scientific purpose, and the scientists present play their part by weighing the swans, taking blood samples and checking for feather lice. It is always a most enjoyable event, though tiring for both swans and those rounding them up! By the time it's over some five or six tonnes of swan will have been picked up, weighed, and returned carefully to freedom in the Fleet.

The heaviest swan ever authenticated came from Germany and

A watercolour by John Fair of a group of Abbotsbury cygnets. A hatch of five, as here, is common at Abbotsbury, although nationally six is more usual.

PREVIOUS PAGE The Swannery in winter, with the Chesil Bank and Lyme Bay in the background.

weighed-in at a massive 47 pounds, but one bred at Abbotsbury about ten years ago comes a close second. From the start he was much bigger than all the other males, or 'cobs', but much less faithful. Within four years he had turned up with three different mates. Few of his young survived because instead of staying with them and protecting them he spent most of his time chasing all the other males. One day he waddled down the path, flopped into the water, spread his wings and died instantly. He had a wing span of 7 feet 10 inches and weighed 42 pounds, a good 12 pounds more than most big cobs. He shared his ring number, 007, with James Bond, and after a post-mortem we found he had died of Avian Tuberculosis.

Because Abbotsbury Swannery has been in existence so long many of the tales told about its inmates are probably apocryphal. One such story dates back to the turn of the century and concerns a swan known as the 'Guardsman'. According to legend, he had a wing span of ten feet and was said to be five feet tall – a size that really would have been intimidating if confronted in the middle of a path! Another such tale is of a pair of swans who returned to Abbotsbury for several years in a row, courted and made a nest, but never produced an egg. It turned out that both were male!

Several years ago we were asked by a farmer to remove a young swan named Cedric from a stream near Dorchester who had been caught molesting lambs. He was of a solitary nature, and once back at Abbotsbury took up residence in the stream outside the wall. When a television company asked how fast a swan can fly, it was decided that Cedric would make the perfect guinea-pig. Posts were set up 200 hundred yards apart, manned by time-keepers with synchronised stop watches. To persuade Cedric to fly in the right direction we waited for the correct wind, put him down-wind at the top of a field and called him from the bottom. It worked first time, and we even filmed his flight. He flew at 24 miles per hour.

My own first encounter with swans took place some eighteen years ago, shortly after arriving at Abbotsbury, and concerned one at Fontmell Magna, a village near Shaftesbury, that was terrorizing the villagers and even attacking cars. The only person it would allow to pass was its owner, who armed herself with a

A swan turning her unhatched eggs.

The hatching period extends from mid-May to the end of June. It is an anxious time, with the swans trying to keep their broods intact and the Swanherd's assistants attempting to keep the families together.

43

rake. Having been asked to take it away, we drove over on a bitter February day. Full of bravado, I stood with a crook on the edge of a low wall near the village pond and waited for it to attack, which it quickly did. I managed to get the crook round its neck, whereupon it turned and flew out over the pond with me still hanging on, to the barely-concealed amusement of the villagers who had turned out to watch the removal of their enemy. This bird was the most aggressive I have ever encountered, and having been dumped waist-deep in icy water my feelings towards it were only slightly mollified by a change of clothes and a welcome tot of whisky.

Swans, I have since learnt, often do what is least expected of them. A pair we supplied to a Somerset country house would allow those visiting the house to enter the outside toilet, then stand guard outside the door and prevent anyone leaving. One bird swam all the way to Alderney, whilst only recently another pair decided to swim across the Fleet, cross Chesil Bank and swim in rough seas to West Bay, nine-and-a-half miles away, followed by their five three-day-old cygnets.

A close up of necks and heads.

Swans flighting in to feed. As the heaviest flying bird, they only take to the wing when necessary or, as here, when tempted by a hand-out of wheat.

Members of Anna Pavlova's 'corps de ballet' dancing 'Swan Lake' on the shore of the Fleet.

Hopefully, such stories give a flavour of what life is like in the Abbotsbury Swannery. Looking after the oldest herd of domesticated swans in the country is a serious business, and the Swannery serves an important educational and scientific purpose. Yet it also gives untold pleasure to those who work there and the thousands of visitors who each year walk amongst the birds. Few can perhaps gain as much as the great ballet dancer Anna Pavlova, who stood on the edge of the Fleet and studied the swans when rehearsing her legendary performance of 'Swan Lake' in 1931.

One of the most remarkable features of the Swannery is that so little has changed since 1393. It may be managed differently, but it can still impart a sense of well-being to our visitors. Walking amongst the nesting sites, it is almost impossible to be unawaware of both the closeness of nature and the Swannery's ancient history.

A great deal of important scientific work is done at the Swannery, and the photograph on the opposite page gives a panoramic view of the 'Round Up', during which all the swans are caught, weighed and checked before being returned to the waters of the Fleet.

Every now and then an escaped bird from a zoo or wildlife park, like the flamingo below, takes up temporary residence amongst the swans, adding an exotic splash of colour.

OPPOSITE PAGE TOP *A group of children with John Fair, who is pointing to the height reached by the floodwater in the Great Gale of 1824.*

OPPOSITE PAGE BOTTOM *The Swannery welcomes tens of thousands of visitors every year, for nowhere else in the world can people enjoy the swan's life-style and behaviour at such close quarters.*

LEFT *Non-breeding swans gratefully accept a hand-out of wheat.*

ABOVE *The Swanherd's assistants checking the number of eggs and cygnets on some of the nests. It is important that the success of every breeding attempt is recorded.*

The Sub-tropical Gardens

The story of Abbotsbury's Sub-tropical Gardens begins almost 250 years ago in 1765 when Elizabeth, the wife of the 1st Earl Ilchester, built a mock castle as a summer residence on a bluff overlooking the Chesil Bank and the open sea. The Castle itself no longer remains. The original was burned down in 1913, and its replacement was demolished in 1934. What does survive however is the nucleus of the original gardens planted by the 1st Countess on the steep slope between the castle and the beach and in a sheltered inland hollow. At first glance Abbotsbury might seem an unlikely site for such an enduring and remarkable garden. Yet there is much in its favour. The hills provide shelter from the coldest winds, an early planting of tamarisk and evergreen oaks breaks the strength of the salt-laden south-westerlies blowing in off the sea, whilst the chances of frost are reduced by the warmth of the deep water off the Chesil Bank, which shelves rapidly. Equally importantly, the heart of the garden lies over Abbotsbury's only area of sandy soil, providing an opportunity to create a garden of unusual interest. Indeed, a grove of acid-loving camellias planted from the original introduction from Japan in 1792 still flowers today. The 125 feet high Caucasian Wing Nut tree is the finest specimen in Europe. A pair of trees similar to the Olive and native to Madeira (*Picconia excelsea*) were planted at Abbotsbury in 1784, and at 60 feet are the tallest in Britain.

The character of the Gardens' owes much to the fact that successive generations of the family have continued to build on what the 1st Countess started. Her grandson, Henry Fox-Strangways, planted the 22 acres of oak, ash, and Scots pine that

Elizabeth, 1st Countess of Ilchester (1723-1792), who first planted the gardens.

OPPOSITE PAGE *The Sunken Lawn framed with magnolia blossom.*

53

The Bothy Garden.

A drawing by Samuel Grimm of Abbotsbury Castle shortly after it was built in 1765.

The Castle built in 1915 to replace the original, but hardly ever lived in due to structural faults and itself demolished in 1934.

form Stavordale Wood to the south-east of the original Walled Garden, giving it protection and a backbone on which to build. This expansion was continued by Henry's successor, William, the 4th Earl, an amateur botanist of distinction and an authority on European flora. His work as a diplomat led to a whole range of carefully selected plants arriving at Abbotsbury from all over the world, many of them wild species that William was the first to cultivate: a genus of small Cotoneaster-like shrubs was named 'Stranvaesia' in his honour. The area between the Walled Garden and Stavordale Wood was planted up in the 1890s when the lily ponds were created and the walks planned. An 1899 catalogue of the Gardens' plants lists over 5000 species, many of them rare shrubs and exotic trees, like the 60 feet Magnolia campbelli that still continues to flower.

Between the gutting of the first castle in 1913 and the late 1960s the Gardens went through a period of decline, aided by two World Wars and the depression in the 1930s. Their rescue was started by Lady Teresa Agnew. Although new plants from Mexico, Nepal and China were planted, much of her work was restoration, a task now being continued by her daughter, the Honourable Charlotte Morrison, particularly since the damage caused by severe storms in 1990.

The Gardens charm derives as much from the numerous smaller gardens inside it as from the plants themselves. The Tea, Rose, Victorian, Valley, Peat and other Gardens are linked by walks designed to combine secrecy and surprise, so that one unfolds into the next. Winding paths criss-cross the valley, whilst small bridges span the stream. There are stepped ponds, lawns and quiet woodland rides, all of them punctuated by deliberate splashes of colour from the azaleas, tree paeonies and hydrangeas that extend the flowering season into early autumn.

The stone-built bothy in the Bothy Garden was built as a home for the gardener once responsible for stoking the boiler that heated the greenhouses. There is a semi-circle of Spanish ships' cannon lifted from Lyme Bay on the West Lawn, as well as the graves of dogs belonging to the family, three of which contain the bodies of the first golden retrievers to be bred. Add peacocks, conservatories, and the occasional glimpses of sea, and it is easy to appreciate what makes the Sub-tropical Gardens so delightful, as well as such a fascinating example of a garden's past.

LEFT *The Victorian Garden, with a tall Chusan palm tree in the centre.*

ABOVE *The azaleas in spring.*

The Reed and Withy Beds

Abbotsbury's thatched cottages are one of its greatest glories. Their honey-coloured roofs with their traditional deep eaves line every lane and alley. Some of the roofs are new, some patched, on another a thatcher might well be precariously balanced, surrounded by bundles of reed. What makes them unique is that they are thatched with reed from Abbotsbury's own beds, just as they have been since time immemorial.

The village's reed and willow beds still play an important part in its seasonal life. Both are mainly grown on the marshy ground surrounding the Swannery, where they also help shelter the nesting swans and provide a wonderful habitat for a whole range of plants, birds and animals.

A mechanical scythe now cuts the 50 or so acres of reed. But it was once hand-cut by about a dozen men, often fishermen glad of winter work, when the swans were feeding at the eastern end of the Fleet. They worked systematically and in lines, each keeping a safe distance from his neighbour's hook. To reduce the dangers, anyone left-handed became a 'strapper', responsible for gathering up two heaped armfuls of reed, and then tying them up into one of several thousand bundles harvested each year – sufficient to thatch a handful of cottages.

Commercial reed beds depend on regular maintenance to keep cropping, as they quickly deteriorate. They dry out if leaves are allowed to accumulate, after which other plants soon invade. Grasses and nettles are followed by scrub willow, sycamore and ash. Within a few years the bed will be overgrown and useless. The ditches have to be kept dug, so that water can be carried to

The village basket-maker in 1925 outside his shop in Back Street: the building still stands.

OPPOSITE PAGE *Reeds on the edge of the Decoy Pond in late autumn.*

Cutting reeds by hand in the 1930s.

the beds in spring to encourage growth and keep weeds at bay. In autumn the flow is reversed. The beds are drained so that the stems can dry out, because reed cut 'green' will eventually rot.

Not all the reed is used for thatching. Several hundreds of bundles are set aside as nesting material for the swans, and some is used in the Duck Decoy to renew the screens lining the tunnels.

This rich mixture of traditional uses is also true of the willow, which still provides the spars, or wooden staples, for fixing the thatch to a roof. But it once supplied the village baker with faggots for his oven, as well as fencing posts and sheep hurdles. There are less withy than reed beds at Abbotsbury, but their management is just as important. The willow is harvested when the shoots, or 'gads', are four or five years old, then halved, split, and made up into bundles.

An exception were the one-year-old rods cut from the coppice beneath St Catherine's Chapel for tying up the bundles of reed. These same unpeeled rods were also sold to the village basket-maker, whose disused shop can still be seen, and whose shelves would once have been lined with lobster pots and game crates, as well as a variety of more workaday baskets. Not all of Abbotsbury's willow is cut each year. By harvesting the beds in a five year rotation a regular crop is sustained. This also benefits the wildlife, in that the differences in growth help add to its diversity. Plants that appear to be dormant suddenly come to life when sunlight penetrates a freshly cut area. Campion, comfry, meadowsweet, primroses and bluebells burst into flower, in turn attracting butterflies, moths and other insects. In their wake come chiffchaffs, willow warblers, dunnocks, wrens and

Here and there amongst the reed and withy beds the rare Southern Marsh Orchid may be found.

A Reed Warbler feeding its young in the Abbotsbury reed beds.

Harvesting the reed for thatching is a winter job for the Swanherd's assistants, 'Dick' Dalley and Dave Wheeler.

Peter Paul annually uses withies from Abbotsbury for hurdle and spar-making.

OPPOSITE PAGE *The coppiced stools of willow in Chapel Withy Bed. The willow is still used for basket-making.*

flycatchers. Dormice skittle through the undergrowth. Roe deer browse on the lush foliage.

Because reed beds are growing scarcer, those at Abbotsbury are now managed in such a way as to encourage wildlife wherever possible. The birds have been the greatest beneficary, and the warblers and buntings that traditionally nest in the reeds now share their nesting sites with one of the rarest of all reed-bed birds, the bearded tit. In the autumn massive flocks of swallows, sand martins and yellow wagtails feed amongst the beds before embarking on their long migrational journey to Africa. As the warm weather visitors go, the winter ones appear. Wailing screams betray the presence of water rails, stonechats flit amongst the withering reed flowers, one eye on the hen-harrier hovering menacingly overhead.

The Duck Decoy

In 1655 the new owner of Abbotsbury, Sir John Strangways, and his son Giles, leased land on the edge of the Fleet to John Hearne of Sherborne for the construction of a duck decoy and a 'little house adjoyneigne'. That same decoy is now nearly 350 years old, and is one of only five still in use in Britain today. Not only is it the oldest working example, but also the one truest to its original design.

The idea of trapping wildfowl by luring them up a wide-mouthed tunnel covered with netting into a bag at the tail of the tunnel is fairly straightforward – and effective. The first surviving records of the Abbotsbury decoy date to 1662 and list 112 duck and teal supplied to the kitchens at Melbury, and the sale of a further 966.

Only two tunnels, or 'pipes', now run from the square decoy pond near the swans' nesting site (though a third one nearby leads directly from the Fleet lagoon). The mesh covering the tunnel is supported by locally-cut ash or willow hoops, and the entire 'pipe' is about 50 metres long. As well as tapering, it is slightly curved so that ducks entering it can't see the fate of their companions at the other end. Tame ducks act as decoys, and grain is used to help entice the wildfowl down the tunnel. Once inside, the duck are driven towards the tail by the decoyman, who appears from behind one of a number of reed screens placed at an angle alongside the tunnel. It sounds simple, but ducks are highly sensitive to the slighest danger and a lot depends on the skill of the decoyman.

Traditionally, the annual haul averaged about 500-600 birds, though in the 1920s 2,564 duck were taken in three seasons.

Most of these were eaten locally, with any surpluses being sent to market in London. All that has since changed, and the wildfowl caught in the Abbotsbury decoy are now ringed and released as a way of learning more about their migrational movements.

Ringing was first started in 1937 on teal and mallard. Other wildfowl since ringed include gadwall, pintail, shoveler, wigeon, pochard and a solitary cinnamon teal. It is hard work, for as well as ringing the birds have to be sexed and measured. But the rewards are immense, as a great deal has been learnt about the life expectancy and means of death of birds caught in the Abbotsbury decoy.

Father and son, Fred and Cecil Lexster, watch ducks nearing one of the 'pipes' in the 1950s.

OPPOSITE PAGE *The Duck Decoy from the air.*

65

They have been found in 14 different countries, ranging from Norway to Russia. Inevitably most are shot, but the most spectacular recording is surely that of a tufted duck whose ring was found in the eyrie of a sea-eagle in Finland? The distances flown by these birds are extraordinary, with both a teal and a wigeon flying more than 4000 kilometres before being shot, one in the Arctic Circle, the other on the Siberian Plain. Nor is their speed any less remarkable, for a teal released at Abbotsbury was caught six hours later in Pembrokeshire, equal to a journey of 500 miles a day. Decoying duck on the edge of the Fleet at Abbotsbury is one of the pleasures of winter, be it at dawn in the face of a chilling easterly or with rain beating in from the south-west under a darkening sky. Ringing and releasing helps us learn more about how best to help these colourful elegant birds survive the problems that now confront them, so that we in turn can look forward to many more centuries of 'working the pipes' of the Abbotsbury decoy.

BELOW *The Decoyman's house, almost destroyed in the Great Gale of 1824, is now a Swannery Information Room.*

RIGHT *Looking out from one of the decoy 'pipes'.*

St Catherine's Chapel, the Fleet and Chesil Bank, with Portland in the distance.

The Chesil Bank and the Fleet

In *Moonfleet,* his classic adventure story of smuggling in 18th century Dorset, the novelist John Meade Falkner described the Fleet as 'a lake of brackish water ... good for nothing except sea-fowl, herons and oysters ... shut off from the open Channel by a monstrous beach or dike of pebbles.'

The 17 mile length of the Chesil Bank combines with the 8 miles of the Fleet to form one of Britain's best-loved coastal landscapes, and one which is geologically unique. Seen from the high ground above Abbotsbury, with the long Fleet lagoon protected to seaward by the 'monstrous beach' of the Chesil, they complete what many consider to be one of England's finest views.

The origins of the Chesil Bank are still debated, but it seems probable that it began with rock debris being washed down by melting water at the end of the last Ice Age into what was then a dry Lyme Bay. As the sea level rose, wave action gathered up the debris and threw it back onto the shore, where the sea's ceaseless pounding gradually rounded the fragments into pebbles.

The Chesil owes its name to the Saxon for shingle, 'cisel'. The prevailing winds are south-westerly, and over the centuries tide and wind have graded the shingle into different sizes along the length of the Bank. Because the larger pebbles offered greater resistance to the waves, they were more readily swept eastward. Thus the pebbles at Portland on the eastern end are potato-sized, whilst at Bridport they are no larger than a pea – allowing those familiar with the area to know where they are even in the dark, a piece of local knowledge once much abused by smugglers landing their cargoes at night!

The Fleet was also created by the last Ice Age, for as the sea level rose it breached the sand bar between Weymouth and Portland, forming a backwater which flooded the low-lying land behind Chesil Bank. The word comes from the Saxon for inlet, 'Fleot', but the name alone does little to hint at the extraordinary richness of the aquatic flora and fauna that flourish in its warm shallow waters. The Fleet's width varies from 110 metres to more than a kilometre. Its mainland shoreline follows a tortuous secretive route around a succession of rounded hills whose small streams empty their mud and silt into the Fleet. The only village along its length, also called Fleet, was a victim of the Great Gale of 1824. For the sea then swept over the Chesil, destroying all but the church chancel and a handful of cottages. The remains of the chancel, lit only by a narrow east window, today stand in a small churchyard fringed with fir trees.

Although the Fleet is still subject to storms, the tide loses its power by about two-thirds of its length. Beyond this the water is 'ponded' and any change of level is caused by its being 'pushed up' by the tidal water entering the Fleet under Ferry Bridge. Rainfall and saltwater percolating through the Chesil Bank also have an impact on the Fleet, and its shallow waters are easily affected by temperature. Ice forms easily in winter, whilst hot summers encourage algae.

At low tide the complicated network of narrow channels that distribute the tidal water around the Fleet become exposed, as do the mud flats. In summer, the flats might easily be mistaken for lawns, as they are then swathed in underwater grasses whose deep roots stop the tide from washing them away. As well as the

four species of grasses, the Fleet boasts more than 150 species of seaweeds, all of which provide sanctuary and food for the fishes, crustaceans, molluscs, sea-anemones and worms with which it abounds. Its birdlife is famous, not just for the swans, but for a whole range of overwintering wildfowl and the waders who pick their way along the foreshore shallows.

To marine scientists, the Fleet's complex ecology is of endless fascination. Nowhere else in the British Isles do so many species successfully co-exist in so many habitats packed into such a small area. The nutrient and chemical balance of the water is frequently monitored. Temperature, salinity and wave movement are studied to see how the Fleet's inhabitants react to the changing conditions.

Apart from its busy mouth, where small boats moor and a modern bridge links Portland to mainland Dorset, the Fleet is a secluded backwater. The only boats that can successfully navigate its shallows and carpets of weed are flat-bottomed trows or troughs. A few fisherman, under licence, net eel and mullet, but fishing is restricted to reduce the impact on wildlife and because the Fleet is a protected bass nursery area.

The only industry is a traditional one – oyster farming. Flint scrapers used by our prehistoric ancestors to prise open shellfish have been found on the shore, but the first commercial oyster farm wasn't started until the 17th century. Although that had closed by the end of the 19th century, a million oysters a year are now being grown in the plankton-rich waters of the Fleet by the Abbotsbury Oyster Farm.

Happily, all other attempts to make the Fleet more productive have been a waste of time. The most spectacular, and costly, took place in 1630 when a wall, with sluices, was built across the lagoon in the vain hope of draining it and creating farmland. Seawater seeping through the Chesil Bank put paid to the

A Sea King helicopter from HMS Osprey lifting a prototype 'bouncing bomb' from the waters of the Fleet in October 1992, exactly fifty years after it was dropped during wartime trials. The bomb's inventor, Barnes Wallis, watched some of the trials from the coastguard cottages in the background. The final bomb was ultimately used in the famous Dam Busters' raid over the Ruhr in 1943.

A section from the 1758 Abbotsbury Estate Map, showing both the Swannery and Duck Decoy. The original map is about eight feet square and is full of glorious details, such as the man o'war in the lower illustration: note the officer with a megaphone on the poop deck bellowing orders at the crew of the ship's boat.

scheme, and its principal investor, Sir George Horsey, was driven by debt into Newgate Prison, where he died a pauper.

The Fleet's tranquillity was also shattered during the Second World War. The threat of invasion produced gun emplacements, pill-boxes, barbed-wire and the 'Dragon's Teeth', two massive rows of concrete cubes that remain Dorset's most substantial wartime relic. In 1942 a Wellington bomber with an apprehensive Barnes Wallis on board flew low over the lagoon before finally releasing an early prototype of what was to become the 'bouncing bomb'.

By contrast, the Chesil Bank is rarely tranquil. It forms the cruellest lee-shore on the southern coast, and the waters off have long been a graveyard for shipping. In *Moonfleet*, Meade Falkner described its impact on a ship driven ashore in a storm: 'And once on the beach, the sea has little mercy, for the water is deep right in, and the waves curl over and fall on the pebbles with a weight no timbers can withstand. Then if the poor fellows try to save themselves, there is a deadly under-tow or rush back of the water, which sucks them off their legs, and carries them again under the thundering waves.' Not for nothing is the eastern end known as Deadman's Bay.

Roman galleys, Spanish galleons and three-decker battleships from the time of Trafalgar have all ended their days on the Chesil. One such casualty was the 350 ton Dutch merchantmen *Hope*, which was blown off course by high winds in thick fog and struck opposite Fleet in 1749. On board was £50,000 in bullion, much of it silver and gold dust. Luckily, the mast snapped and fell onto the beach, allowing the crew to clamber to safety. The first looters arrived at dawn. As news of the cargo spread, the crowd grew. At one stage it was estimated that more than 10,000 people, from throughout Dorset, had gathered in search of plunder. Some formed gangs and wore different colours to identify the villages from which they had come. One man was stabbed to death and hastily buried in a shallow grave amidst the pebbles, others died of exposure. It took ten days for troops to disperse the mob, many of whom had drunk themselves into a stupour on the spirits washed ashore with the wreckage. Fog and high winds were also the cause of the worst disaster ever known on the Chesil, the loss of six ships and 298 lives from a convoy of

A rescue harness being used to bring ashore passengers from the Royal Adelaide, *wrecked on the Chesil Bank in 1872. Seven of the passengers on board went down with the ship, but at least five of those who gathered to loot died of drunkenness and exposure.*

merchantmen and military transports in 1795. Once again, looting was widespread, as it was nearly a century later when the 1,385 ton *Royal Adelaide* rolled broadside onto the breakers during a November night in 1872.

The iron-built clipper was outward bound for Australia with a crew of thirty and thirty-nine emigrants on board when it turned back to seek shelter from a south-westerly gale. After grounding,

a group of Portlanders, linked by ropes, managed to get a line aboard. All but seven were taken off before the line snapped. By dawn the handful of men and women left huddled on the poop had been washed overboard and the *Royal Adelaide* had broken up and sunk.

With no one left to save, the crowd turned its attention to the cargo. Hats, soap, candles, cotton, coffee and a solitary pig were followed by casks of rum, brandy and cheap gin. Some men buried their spoils beneath the shingle, others risked drowning dragging the casks from the surf. Again, drunkenness led to deaths from exposure, and the final death toll of five was only two less than those who perished off the ship.

Happily, not all the wrecks on the Chesil have ended so tragically. During the Great Gale of 1824 a 100 ton sloop, the *Ebenezer*, was washed so far up the beach that its crew were able to jump to safety and the vessel was later hauled down the other side of the Bank and relaunched into Portland Harbour. Even though it took place a hundred and seventy years ago the Great Gale remains one of those legendary Dorset events by which all others are measured. A 22 feet pole in the Swannery still marks the height of the flood water as shown by seaweed left draping on the nearby ash tree.

Of course there are summer days when it is hard to imagine what conditions are like on the Chesil Bank during a storm. Although the shingle is constantly shifting, the leeward side is relatively stable. Sea campion, sea carrot, sea pea and the lovely yellow-horned poppy thrive in the chinks between pebbles. Those same pebbles help camouflage the eggs of the little and common terns, and provide a roost for huge numbers of gulls. The patient observer may well be rewarded by seeing a hare or roe deer swim across the Fleet to browse on the marine grasses and lichens at the back of the Bank, whilst foxes and hedgehogs make occasional raids with their young in search of prey and carrion.

The Chesil's richest harvest are the shoals of mackerel who appear off the Bank every spring. The mackerel are still netted in the traditional way, helped by an open rowing boat called a 'lerret', which is built double-ended so it can easily be launched and landed. The mackerel are caught using a long seine net which is rowed out in a semi-circle from the shore and pulled in by hand.

Until recently, Abbotsbury was very much a fishing village, and the first sighting of the mackerel by the look-out posted on St Catherine's Hill was an important event. On Old May Day (May 13th) the children of each boat crew made a garland of flowers, which were then taken out in the boats and thrown into the sea as an offering.

Most of the fish caught off the Chesil today are cod and conger taken by the many anglers who line the shore – all of which seems a far cry from the 11th century charter granting the abbot 'all things driven by the sea to the shore, wreck and great fish.' The ownership of the Chesil Bank passed from the abbot to the Strangways family in the 16th century, and the Ilchester Estate is still responsible for its management. The other principal land-owner is the Crown, for Portland is a Royal Manor. The boundary stone between the two still exists. As Portland's only boundary it has been carefully guarded for centuries in the time-honoured way of 'beating the bounds'. Even today, a young Portlander is ceremoniously caned on the bound-stone every seven years.

It may seem odd that a pebble beach the length of the Chesil has to be 'managed', but it is too internationally important to be left alone. In pre-motorcar days it was a remote beach visited by only a few local fishermen. The number of visitors has increased substantially in recent years, threatening its fragile flora and fauna. Until recently shingle was extracted. Two violent storms in 1979 and 1989 noticeably reduced its height and breath in certain places, raising fears that it might yet be breached. Time and money have to be spent clearing the Bank of the drums of chemicals, plastic debris and other flotsam that are the modern equivalent of 'wreck driven ashore'. Yet despite such threats, the Chesil remains one of Britain's most remarkable lengths of coastline. A 17th century traveller called it the 'stranger's wonder, the nation's boast' – a description that still fits it today.

The ancient ferry at Smallmouth was Portland's only practical link with the mainland until the building of the first bridge in 1839.

Some traditions resist all change. A hundred years separate the photograph above and the one on the opposite page of freshly-caught mackerel being sorted and packed on the beach.

Garland Day in Abbotsbury. On Old May Day the children of each boat crew made a garland of flowers, which was then taken out in the boats and thrown into the sea as an offering.

LEFT *Anglers fishing off the Chesil Bank in high seas. The waters off the Bank are famous for conger, cod, bass and halibut.*

ABOVE *Tending eel nets in the calmer waters of the Fleet.*

RIGHT *Mature oysters being taken from the Abbotsbury Oyster Farm racks at Ferry Bridge. A million oysters a year are now harvested from the plankton-rich waters of the Fleet.*

An aerial view of the entire Fleet, with the Swannery in the foreground and Portland lying low against the horizon.

LEFT *Wind and tide have driven the largest pebbles on Chesil Bank to its eastern end.*

RIGHT *A carpet of sea-pink or thrift on the shoreward side of the shingle, with the Fleet in the distance.*

LEFT *The chancel of old Fleet church, all that remains of the village destroyed in 1824 during the Great Gale when the sea broke through the Chesil Bank.*

RIGHT *A Ringed Plover on its nest on the Chesil, and a pair of Little Terns feeding their young.*

This red and white trow with Don Moxom on board was one of six specially built by the Earl of Ilchester in 1904 for a visit by Edward VII.

84

Acknowledgements

We would like to thank the following for their help, support and encouragement. Without it, this book would not have been possible. Abigail Adams, Allen Arnold, Ashley Arnold, Maureen Attwooll (Weymouth Library), Greg Ayles, Ernie Ayles, Jeannie Bailey, I. D. Beale Esq for the photograph of Abbotsbury Station, Steve Belasco for the photograph of the Sea King helicopter lifting the 'bouncing bomb', Mervyn and Mary Bown (Abbotsbury Sign Studio), Louise Cookson, Neville Copperthwaite, Wayne Copperthwaite, Bet Dalley, Dick Dalley, Roy Dalley, Dorset County Museum, the Dorset Natural History and Archaeological Society for permission to reproduce the photograph of Anna Pavlova's 'corps de ballet', Dorset Records Office, Darren Ellis, Yvonne Fair, Les and Rosie Gardner, Adrian Graham, Edward Green and the staff of the Ilchester Estate Office, Stephen Griffiths, Steve Groves, John Harbige, John Hayman, Nell Humpherstone, Cecil Lexster, Peter Limm, Ted Millbank, Audrey Minors, Liz and Edgar Moxom, Peter Nicol, Peter Paul, Don Peach, Andy Poore, Richard Pullen, Steve Packham for the photograph of the Reed Warblers, Eric Ricketts for the watercolour reconstruction of the Abbey, Roger and Lindy Ross-Turner, the Reverend Phillip Seale, Graham Shaw for the map, Mollie Slatter, Merle Stean, Peter Thornton for the lettering in the translation of the Court Roll, Reg Trevett, Eddie Trigg, John, Cheryl and Tom Varley (H & R Design), Roger Wayne, Dave Wheeler, Dave, Wendy and Samantha Wood (Woodcoate Stud).

The Authors

John Fair spent the first half of his adult life teaching craft and design, but was always interested in wildlife and conservation. He joined the Swannery staff in 1974 as Fleet Warden and was appointed Swanherd two years later. He is the author of *The Mute Swan*, published in 1985 and illustrated with his own watercolour studies of the swans at Abbotsbury.

Don Moxom was born and educated in Dorchester. He joined the Swannery staff in 1976 after short spells in the Army and commerce, and is now the Warden of the Chesil Bank and the Fleet Nature Reserve.

Peyto Slatter began taking photographs as a medical student. He served in the Royal Air Force during the war and has recently retired as a practising doctor. He has spent the last two years taking the photographs for this book, mostly using a Rolleiflex camera and a variety of lenses, ranging from a 55 mm wide-angle shift lens to a 1000 mm telephoto.